THREE
CLUB
JUGGLING

THREE CLUB JUGGLING

AN INTRODUCTION

DICK FRANCO

brian dubé, inc.

DESIGNED BY BERNARD SCHLEIFER
Published in the United States by Brian Dube,Inc.
Manufactured in the United States of America

Library of Congress Cataloging-in-Publication Data
Franco, Dick, 1952-
    Three club juggling.

    1. Juggling. I. Zemaitis, Ann. II. Dube, Brian. III. Title
GV1559.F73   1987   793.8   87-30370
ISBN 0-917643-02-X Paperback
ISBN 0-917643-03-8 Hardcover

First Printing October, 1987
Second Printing May, 1993
Third Printing November, 1995

This book is dedicated to the memory of Ludwig Mayer, also known as Bobby May, the International Juggler.

Bobby May

ACKNOWLEDGMENTS

Joe Sullivan
Paul Bachman
Ken Benge
El Gran Picaso
Kris Kremo

CONTENTS

Dick Franco being presented the "Silver Clown Award" by Princess Grace of Monaco, 7th Monte Carlo Circus Festival, 1980

FOREWORD

Welcome to the world of club juggling. It may appear bewildering at first as many paths open up before you. What you need is someone to guide you.

Dick Franco has travelled this path and it has led him to worldwide fame. Along the way, he has won the silver clown award at the 7th Monte Carlo Circus Festival and was a gold medal winner at the 1979 and 1985 Circus World Championships in London. As a performer, master juggler, and instructor, I can think of no one better to guide you on this path.

How far you travel is up to you, but with this manual at your side the going will be easier. It reflects a decade's thinking and will be a giant step forward in your progress.

In just a few minutes, as you continue reading this manual, you will begin to feel confident about your progress as a club juggler. Relax and enjoy it. All the best jugglers have had guides and you will be continuing in a great tradition.

Juggling is a science that requires know how and perserverence. The knowledge and confidence you gain will lead the way. Follow it. It's the path to your success. There are still new worlds for you to conquer.

Dennis Soldati
New York, November 1986

"The Great Juggling Jacobie Brothers" Dick Francis and Joe Sullivan 1970

ABOUT THE AUTHOR

Dick Franco is a world renowned juggler who, in the past eight years, has performed in nearly every major entertainment capital of the world. At the time this book was written, he held the official title of "World Champion", which was awarded to him at the "Circus World Championships" competition in London, England in 1979. It was there that Dick scored an upset victory over juggling greats, Kris Kremo and Rudi Schweitzer, after only four years as a professional.

In 1980, Dick went on to Europe to appear in the prestigious Monte Carlo Circus Festival, hosted by Prince Ranier of Monaco. Dick again surprised the star-studded judges and received top honors when presented the "Silver Clown Award" by Princess Grace, an honor thus far achieved by only two other jugglers, Kris Kremo in 1981 and Sergei Ignatov in 1983.

Dick started juggling at the age of 20, when he was taught by long-time friend, Joe Sullivan. Together they formed an act called "The Juggling Jackobie Brothers", which performed locally for a number of years. In 1974, Dick discovered the I.J.A. (International Jugglers Association) and attended his first convention in Sarasota, FL. He was elected president, and ran the 1975 Youngstown, Ohio convention, a convention that set the precedent for the huge juggling conventions of today. He was the winner of the three-club competition there.

The main force behind Dick's career has always been his close friendship with juggling legend Bobby May. It was Bobby May who gave him inspiration and confidence to become a professional juggler. Bobby often referred to Dick as "The Wonder Boy of Juggling" because he learned so fast, juggled so smoothly and made it to the top of the European show business circuit faster than anyone on record.

Dick Franco, thirty two at the time this was written, is currently a highly active professional juggler, most recently making appearances throughout Europe, in Las Vegas, Reno, Atlantic City as well as on ABC TV's "That's Incredible".

Dick's favorite jugglers are Bobby May, Kris Kremo, Gran Picaso, Sergei Ignatov and Paul Bachman.

INTRODUCTION

Of the basic juggling props, clubs are considered to be the most difficult with which to learn the basic juggling patterns. Not only must the club be thrown accurately to the catching hand, but also the correct rotation of the handle is required in order to complete the catch. Although more difficult and frustrating to learn at first, you will probably find club juggling in general more relaxing than any other type of juggling because of the great number of easy variations that can be performed once the mechanics of the basic moves have been mastered. Because of the length, weight and balance of a club, you will find that most of the work is done by the club itself when released at the proper moment during the juggle.

This book will deal with a group of closely related moves that can be perfected in a few months time with two to three hours of practice daily.

Important Suggestions

For about the first two weeks, or at least until the basic cascade pattern is well under control, it is advisable to practice in short sessions, many times per day, such as 20-minutes six times per day. As your endurance and concentration improve, increase the length of your sessions and decrease their number until you arrive at a schedule that is comfortable for you, yet still demonstrates that you are making definite progress from week to week.

Most sports are performed right or left handed. This is definitely not the case with juggling. The worst enemy of a juggler is his "bad side". Therefore, it is of great importance to over practice one's "bad side" in order to make the most efficient progress. It is advisable to warm up the bad side first and spend as much time as is necessary per move to allow equal control to both sides.

Progress among jugglers varies greatly from person to person. A move that is mastered by one juggler in a few days may take weeks for another juggler to learn. Many professional jugglers have spent many hours per day for several years to get a particular stage act ready. For the beginner, visible progress should occur at least every third day. Sometimes a particular move may show little progress after many of days hard practice. Often, a trick like this may come easily if left alone for a week or so.

Choosing a Good Prop

Without the correct props, practice is a waste of time. Therefore, it is imperative that you obtain a prop that will serve you during the beginning stages, as well as carry you through to advanced juggling.

A wide selection of clubs and other juggling supplies is available from the publisher of this book. I suggest you write to him for a free catalog:

Brian Dube, Inc. 520 Broadway, New York, NY 10012

Brian Dube has been a manufacturer of juggling equipment for over twelve years. I have known him for many years and can highly recommend his equipment.

It is advisable for the solo juggler to obtain at least four matched clubs and rotate them during the beginning stages to insure uniform wear. If you are learning with a friend, be sure to get at least 7 matched clubs, as inevitably you will learn to pass 6 and 7 clubs between the two of you.

ONE

Learning How To Juggle Three Clubs

Holding the Club

In the beginning stages the club should be gripped in about the same area of the club for both the throw and the catch as shown in figures 1, 2 & 3.

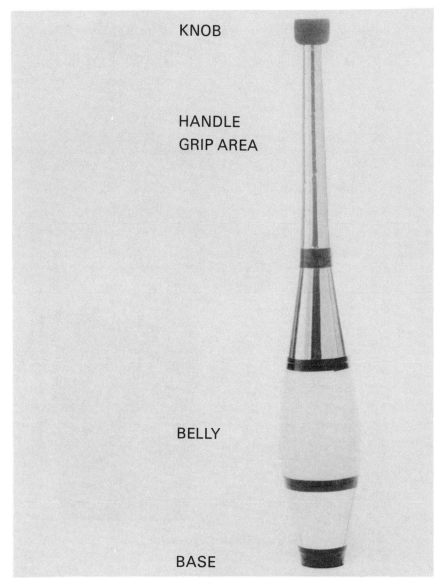

KNOB

HANDLE
GRIP AREA

BELLY

BASE

Figure 1.

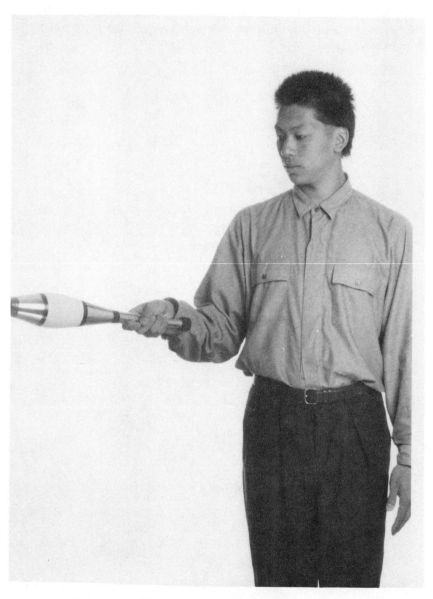

Figure 2. Throw Grip (*Right*)

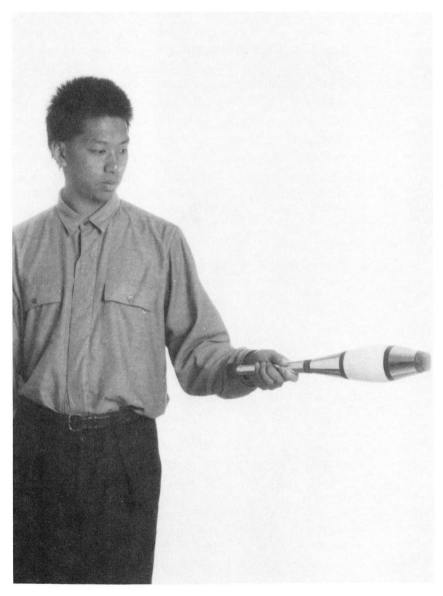

Figure 3. Catch Grip (*Left*)

The club should not be thrown or caught by the knob or too near the belly.

Basic One Club Throws and Catches

The first throw will be a front cross from hand to hand using a single turn of the club. You will start with the club in your right hand, shoulders square, elbows turned out. The club will lay in your loosely gripped hand in line with your thumb and forearm. Throwing arm thumb should be up. Catching arm should remain in an equally opposite position with palm of hand up and open,

Figure 4. Throw Position.

as shown in figure 4. All throws and catches should be made at waist level.

Note that club points left, not straight ahead, and is in line with the right forearm.

The single spin will be accomplished by a slight flick of the wrist just before the club is released so that the club makes one revolution and is caught by the handle in the opposite hand.

The club should pass slightly above eye level and land in your left hand, base pointing left, however on the catch the club should land at a forty-five degree angle to the left forearm.

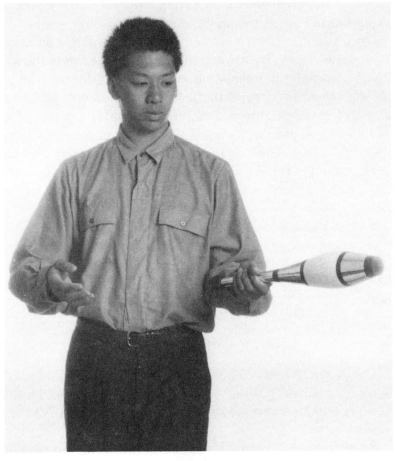

Figure 5.

Note: The club is now at a forty-five degree angle to the left forearm and parallel to the right forearm.

Once the catch is made, roll your left hand over so that the thumb is up and the club is in line with your forearm, once again in the throwing position. Now flex your wrist to dip the base of the club slightly and throw back to your right hand. Don't forget to change from the firm catching grip to a loose, more flexible throwing grip as you roll your hand over.

Throw the club from hand-to-hand until you can do it easily and accurately. Remember to keep the elbows well out and and the shoulders square at all times. Varying the height of throws from a low quick spin to a high slow spin will help improve your control. If you are having trouble catching the club, be sure that the position of the throwing hand is correct.

Once you can control a front cross with a single spin, try it with a double spin. Try to keep the height of the throw the same as with a single spin. Follow the rotation of the double with your eye and count each revolution: 1,2. The club should hit your hand on the count of two. Catching by sight is a good habit to develop as you will clearly see if a club is over or under turned. Therefore, you will be able to compensate by raising or lowering your catching hand. If a club needs to be caught high or low, be sure to return to the waist-high throwing position for the next throw.

Repeat these exercises with 3 and 4 spins and then mix the spins between hands. 1 spin from right, 3 spins from left, 2 spins from right, 1 spin left, 3 spins right, 2 spins left, etc., etc. Three and four spins may need to be thrown higher than a single or double.

Two Clubs

The next exercise will be the front cross wih two clubs or the "two club cascade". When objects cross symetrically in front of the body and land in opposite hands, this is called a "cascade" pattern.

Starting position is the same as in lesson one, but with both hands in the throw position.

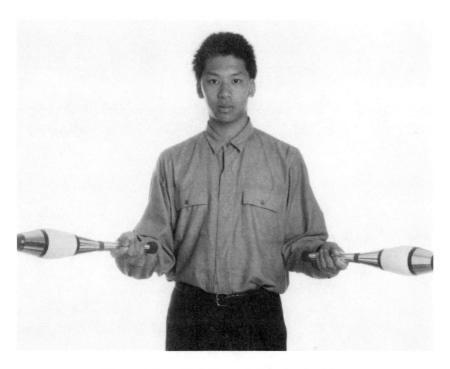

Figure 6. Two-Club Cascade Starting Position.

The first exercise will start with a throw from the right hand to the left. The throw should go no higher than just above eye level. When the club reaches its highest point, just as it starts downward, throw the club from your left hand to your right. As you release, it will be time to catch the first club in your left hand. Just after your make the catch with your left hand it will be time to catch the second club in your right hand. Stop.

Now you should have one club in each hand. They should be in the catching position at a forty-five degree angle to your forearm.

Return both hands to the throwing position once again and repeat the exercise, starting with both right and left hands. Repeat until throws are accurate and both sides of the pattern are equal and opposite.

The next step will be to try to maintain continuous throws and catches from both hands. When the 2-club cascade is done

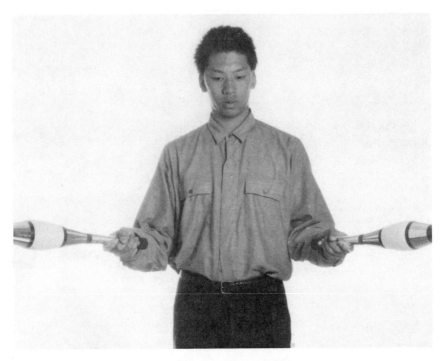

Figure 7. Two-Club Cascade Catching Position.

properly, the sound of the clubs hitting your hands should create a continuous rhythm. Starting with one club in each hand, the throwing sequence should start like this — Right, Left Left, Right Right, Left Left, Right Right, Left Left, and so on.

Every right throw is caught in the left and immediately thrown back to the right, as is every throw from the left caught and immediately thrown back from the right.

Remember that after you make each catch you must roll your hand back to the throwing position. Otherwise, the club will not be in a good catching position when it reaches your opposite hand.

Once you get the cascade going for a few throws, you will find that because of the great amount of concentration you are giving to the throws and catches, you tend to forget to keep your elbows out. This is normal and acceptable, but as your cascade improves, give more thought to your elbows, as it will be an important factor in developing a good three club cascade.

Also, as your two club cascade improves, you will notice that as you throw—left left—or—right right— your opposite hand is doing nothing for a slight moment. As you practice, make yourself aware of each hand at this moment as in this free space you will later fit the third club in.

Once your cascade is consistent with single spins, try it with doubles, and then with triples, and then try this exercise: Four throws singles—four throws doubles—four throws triples— four throws doubles—four throws singles—Stop. When you have obtained fairly good control of this, go on to the next lesson.

Three Clubs

If you have practiced the first two lessons thoroughly, you should be ready to learn the three-club cascade. At first, it will seem like everything is happening very fast and that the air is full of clubs, but soon everything will slow down and you will be able to tell one club from the other.

The first problem you have is where to put the third club when starting out. For the moment, begin with the two clubs in right hand and the third in the left. The right hand grip must be altered to accommodate the extra club. Starting position of the right hand will look like fig.8A.

As in all cascade juggling, you start from the hand holding the most objects. So, in this case the first club to be thrown will be the inner right hand club. Try either method of holding two clubs in one hand and select that which you find the most comfortable and gives you the least difficulty releasing. The author prefers the method shown in fig.8A while many jugglers prefer that shown in fig.8B.

First, practice the release of the inner right hand club. Start with two clubs in the right hand and nothing in the left. Grip the inner club using the tips of the fingers and thumb. with elbows out and throwing angle correct, throw the inner club to the left hand. Repeat this throw with single, double, and triple spins

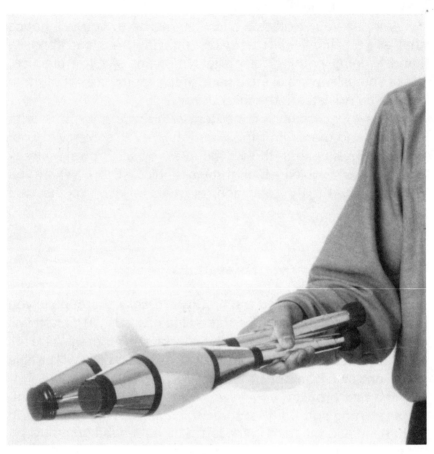

Figure 8a

Note: The knob of the inner right hand club is under the knob of the outer right hand club.

Figure 8b

The knob of the inner right hand club is started above the knob of the outer right hand club.

until it feels comfortable, then repeat the exercise with two clubs in the left and nothing in the right. Lefthand starting position should look like this.

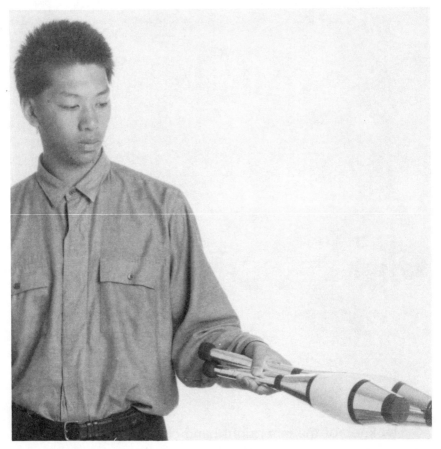

Figure 9a

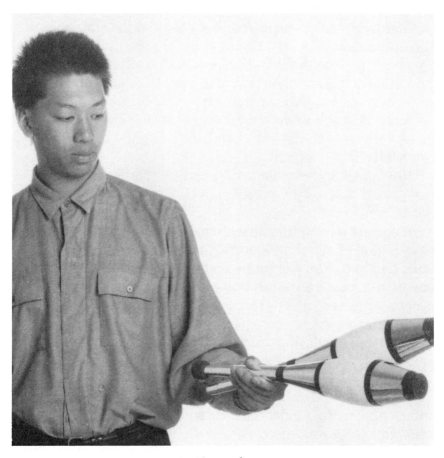

Figure 9b

Repeat the left hand starting throw with single, double and triple spins, until it feels equal to the right.

Since we have practiced the throw with two clubs in one hand, it would be good to learn the catch with two clubs as well before trying the actual cascade.

Like before, start with two clubs in the right hand. Throw the inner club to the left hand and catch it. Then throw the outer club to the left hand and catch it. The second club should be caught so that the clubs return to the starting position.

Repeat this exercise with single, double and triple spins until you are confident with both hands. You should now be ready for the three club cascade.

Start with two clubs in your right hand in the starting position and one in your left. Count your throws starting with the right hand for two throws—right-left. Catch left—catch right—stop. Repeat this and then switch to a left hand start and throw: left—right—catch right—catch left—stop. Repeat.

Next, go back to your right hand starting position and try three throws: Right—left—catch left—right—catch right—catch left—stop. Repeat.

Next, back to right hand start and try four throws: Right—left—catch left—right—catch right—left—catch left—catch right—stop.

If you are having trouble with this, I would suggest that you have a friend help you by putting the clubs through their patterns by hand. You will throw and catch in slow motion while your friend moves the clubs slowly through the air for you. With everything slowed down you can better understand sequence of throws and catches.

If you are not having trouble you can now juggle three clubs.

CONGRATULATIONS.

With four throws and the finish catch under control you should now try for longer runs. Be sure your position is good to start and go for as many throws as you can. Disregard the catch/finish. Juggle until you drop one. Be sure to count your throws. Give each club a number as you throw them, (say from 1 to 10). This will allow you to identify where trouble spots are by the throw number. Once you can consistently get past 20 throws you will be good enough that there will be no need to count the throws any longer.

If you find yourself walking or chasing after the clubs while juggling, STOP. This is one of the worst habits you can develop. Your goal is to control the clubs, not for them to control you. If walking becomes a problem, practice facing a wall. Eventually you will get tired of running into the wall and will learn to juggle correctly.

If walking is the problem, it is likely that you are releasing the clubs too early and throwing them out instead of up. Put your primary concentration on the club you are throwing, and memorize the exact point of release. As soon as the club leaves your hand, switch your concentration to the next throw. Keep your concentration on the club until it has completely left your hand.

Once you have a consistent 20 throws or more, it will be time to go back to the basic throw and catch positions and clear up the technique. Also, I will give you a few exercises to practice that will smooth out your cascade and improve your consistency.

First, try to find a large mirror in front of which to practice. This will be very helpful in improving your technique and balance of the pattern. Start your cascade. Once you have fair control, push your elbows out gradually, as far as you possibly can. The pattern should get lower and wider, and you will find you have to put a little more wrist action on the clubs to get them to rotate. Remember to take note of the sound/tempo of the clubs hitting your hands. Try to force the pattern as wide and low as possible. From this position bring the pattern back in and try to gradually change to a high, slow, narrow pattern with elbows at your sides. When you can change from low and wide, to high and narrow, and back again, your cascade should be good and you can relax by dropping your elbows to whatever you find to be most comfortable for you.

If you happen to experience catching or throwing problems, go back and make sure your position is good and that the height and width of your throws are the same for both left and right.

Now try these variations:

1. Cascade singles: occasionally throwing one high slow single spin from either hand, and then back to cascade.

2. Cascade singles: gradually throw each club higher and slower, single spin, then gradually back down to a normal cascade.

3. Cascade singles: suddenly go into three throws—high, slow, single spins, then suddenly drop back down into a normal cascade.

Try these same variations with double and triple spins, then mix them as you like. Practice hard until you are comfortable with most of these, then go on to Chapter 2.

Tips to Improve Your Basic Cascade

Try: Walking Backwards and Forwards
Running Backwards and Forwards
Turning Left and Right
Kneeling or Jumping Up and Down
Jumping Side to Side
Sitting

TWO

Basic Three Club Tricks

Single Spins

Next we will learn some basic three club tricks, even if you don't have a 100% solid three club cascade, by all means try to make whatever progress possible towards learning the following tricks. I am sure you will find that by attempting these tricks, you will greatly improve your cascade.

If you are already a fair ball juggler, in the coming weeks you will begin to realize just how much more difficult club juggling is. Progress comes at a slower rate, because you now have the length of the club and also the rotation of the handle to contend with. In the next two chapters I will outline ten basic tricks for you, using single spins, some double spins, and then some starting and finishing moves.

Once you have learned everything, you will have the beginnings of a complete professional three club routine, which can be practiced as well as performed as an orderly routine. As you progress further as a club juggler, you can then substitute more advanced tricks for their basic counterpart and not interrupt the basic format. I have followed this method since the very early days of my career and even after eight years as a professional, still find it useful.

The ten basic tricks will be:

1. Under the leg
2. Behind the back
3. Two Clubs in one hand
4. One-Up, Two-Up
5. Reverse Spins
6. No Spin or Flat throw
7. Under the Arm
8. Dips
9. Overhead throw cascade
10. Overhead throw lateral

Please note that all these except for #3 and #4 can be done "full shower", i.e.-every throw from both the right and the left hand is done as a trick throw. With some tricks, however, this may take months of practice once the basic trick is mastered by both hands separately.

Tricks 2,3,4,9 and 10 can and should be learned with double spins once single spins are reasonably mastered. Just follow the same progression given for single spins using doubles and build to random double spins from both sides, eventually leading to continuous double spins from the right, then the left, and finally continuous double spins from both sides.

Under the Leg

Starting with one club only in the right hand, throw it under the right leg to a catch in the left hand. Then, throw it under the left leg to catch it in the right hand and stop.

Repeat this many times until you are comfortable with the throw and catch both sides. Be careful not to throw the club too far in front of you or back into your face. As you throw under your leg, your entire hand should come into view just as you release the club. The club should not touch the back of your leg at any time.

Figure 10. Under-the-Leg, throw position.

Now, try to make ten continuous left and right throws with little or no pause between each. The end result should be the club traveling through this pattern in a smooth, non-stop manner.

Now, take a second club. With one club in each hand, raise your right heel slightly off the ground and shift your weight to your left foot. Throw the left club to the right hand catch. As it leaves your hand, raise the right leg and throw the right club under your right leg to a left hand catch.

Repeat this until you can do it ten times non-stop. Then reverse the process for the left leg throws. Remember to always over practice your bad side. Once you have control of both sides, try alternating left and right for 10 throws.

Now, take the third club and begin your cascade counting each right hand throw. Try to throw the right throw under the right leg. You should shift your weight to the left and get your right heel up off the ground. The leg should begin to raise on $4\frac{1}{2}$ and the throw will be on the count of 5. Your next left will be the first throw of the new cascade, which should keep going. If you are having trouble getting rid of the throw after the under the leg throw, then the under the leg throw should be made a bit higher to give you more time.

Practice this until you have fair control and can maintain the cascade after the under the leg throw. Then, reverse the process for the left side. Work hard until you have consistent, random throws, from both sides.

Behind the Back

This trick is slightly more difficult to learn than the under the leg because the grip for the throw behind the back is different than the catch preceding it. You have only a fraction of a second to catch the club, change grips and then throw.

We will start first by learning the new grip which will release the club behind your back.

The importance of the knob on your clubs will become clear as you learn this trick.

Place the club in the right hand and grip it loosely with the thumb holding the knob as shown in Figure 11.

Figure 11. Behind the back throw grip.

The club should be held loosely enough so that it can pivot slightly at the point where your thumb comes in contact with the knob.

Now extend your right arm so that from the rear it is in the four o'clock position, as in Figure 12.

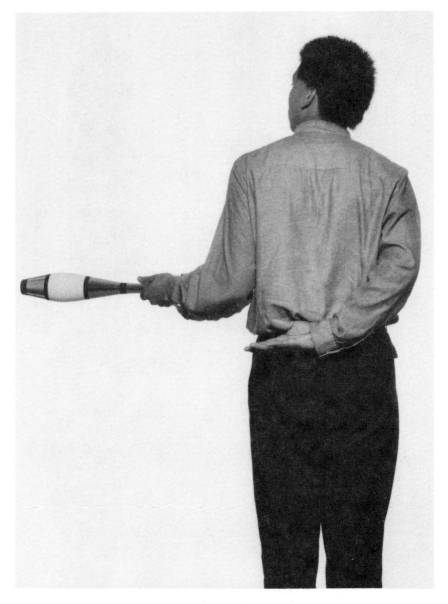

Figure 12.

Gently throw the club, not more than head high, behind the back with one turn so that it edges around the tip of your left shoulder and lands comfortably in your left hand, slightly in front of you with your left arm slightly bent, as shown in Figure 13.

Figure 13. Behind the back catch position.

The club should be caught mid-handle as you would catch during a normal cascade.

If the club flies far away from you to the left, you are releasing too early. If it comes too close to your head, you are releasing too late.

Practice this throw both left and right until you are comfortable with it.

Now, start with the club in the normal cascade throwing position in the left hand. Throw the club in front of you to a normal catch in the right hand. As you catch, let your right arm extend out and down. At the same time, slide the club in your hand from the cascade catch grip to the behind the back throw grip to the behind the back throw grip. Then continue with the back throw to the left hand catch and stop.

Reverse this method for the left side and practice until you can do both directions for ten throws in one continuous, smooth action without moving your feet.

Now take two clubs, one in each hand, both in the normal cascade catch position. Throw left to right in front of you, as you begin the throwing motion with the left start the right hand toward the four o'clock back throw position and grip change flowing directly into the back throw. The left throw should release first with the right back throw releasing a split second later. The right catch is then followed by the left.

You will find the timing of this trick to be the same as the under the leg trick.

Again, reverse this method for your left side and practice until you can do both directions for ten throws in one continuous smooth motion without moving your feet.

Now take all three clubs and begin your cascade. This time we will count both right and left throws starting right. The ninth throw will be a back throw; but, I want you first to put your concentration on the eighth throw, which will be from your left hand. Hint: As you cascade towards the eighth throw, shift the pattern to the right side of your body. The eighth throw should be slightly higher and slower than all the rest. This will give you a little more time to complete the back throw. As you get better with practice, the back throw will become quicker and you will no longer need to slow down the preceding throw. Practice hard until you have good control of random throws, both right and left.

The under the leg and behind the back trick probably seem very difficult to you. THEY ARE very difficult, especially when trying to do them left and right. Don't be discouraged. I have given you these two tricks first, as I believe that they have the greatest effect on improving the amount of control you have over your basic cascade, which will make much easier for you to learn the rest of the tricks in this book. So even though you have not mastered all versions of under the leg and behind the back, by all means go onto other things, but try to give extra attention to tricks one and two until they are mastered.

Juggling Two Clubs in One Hand

Learning to juggle two clubs in each hand is extremely important. Not only does it allow you to do what you wish with your opposite free hand (which is very important for comedy moves), it is also a necessity for learning four clubs later on.

We will first try juggling two clubs with the right hand, single spins, with the clubs remaining in place. Start with two clubs in the right hand as if to start a cascade. The inner club will be thrown first, straight up in the center of your body. The throw should be slow turning and peak about a foot overhead as the first club peaks. The second club will be thrown to the right of the first club. Each club will remain in place and travel straight up and down in columns. The hand will move side to side to catch. Practice this on the right side until you have a consistent pattern.

Reverse the process for the left hand. The inner club being thrown up the center of the body and the second club off to the left.

Remember to keep the clubs in place and the throws fairly high and slow turning. The tendency after the third or fourth throw will be for the throws to get shorter and the turns to get faster. If this happens, remember to push the club out of the palm of your hand leaving the palm open and facing up. There is very little wrist action in this trick as most of the turning action on the club comes from the fingers.

Once learned with single spins, you can move to two in one hand with double spins. This is an essential basic skill since four clubs is generally done with double spins(two clubs in each hand). The greater height and time created by using double spins makes it somewhat easier. Learn to do this in columns as you did with single spins and in outward circles. To do circles with doubles: Starting with two clubs in the right hand, throw the inside club first with a double spin up and slightly to the right. The next club is thrown the same way, bringing it slightly to the left before throwing(to clear the way for the club coming down). The right hand moves back to the right to catch the first club. Continue in the same manner: each club is caught to the right, brought slightly to the left, thrown with a double spin to the right and the right hand move back to the right to catch. Thus the clubs trace a circular path from inside to outside.

Repeat the process with the left hand reversing directions and remembering to throw from the inside and catch on the outside.

Please note that this circle pattern is generally not done with single spins due to the increased difficulty of clearing the clubs in the tighter, lower pattern.

One Up/Two Up

The first use you will have for your two clubs in one hand trick will be in learning the one up/two up trick.

This trick is very valuable to the performing juggler, as to an audience it looks drastically different when compared to most cascading tricks. In short, although the audience does not know exactly what you are doing, when they see one up/two up, they can definitely tell that you are doing something different than before.

We will start with two clubs in the right hand, in the two in one hand start position, and holding the third club in the left hand.

Figure 14.

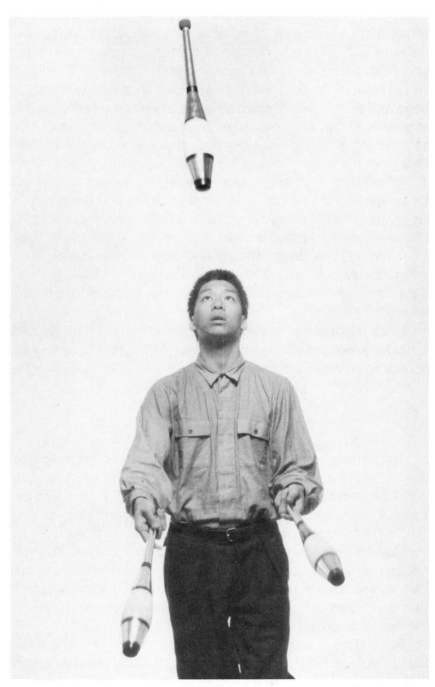

Figure 15.

You will start by throwing the inner right hand club up the center of the body with a high, slow turn. As the first club peaks, the right and left hand clubs are thrown in unison straight up on either side of the first club. These two clubs are thrown in unison and in place. The descending single club is caught in the right hand and is immediately thrown straight back, up between the two outer clubs. The two outer clubs are then caught with the left and right hands, and the now descending single club is caught as the second club in the right hand. Stop.

Repeat this short move until you are fairly confident, then go for longer runs. You will soon realize that all you are doing is juggling two clubs with your right hand while throwing one club, (the same club) , up and down with your left.

Once you can do ten throws and stop, reverse the process and do the same, starting with two clubs in the left hand and the right hand will be throwing one club, the same club, up and down.

Once mastered with singles hands you can work on double spins as described above under "Two In One Hand", doing all double spins with both hands.

Reverse Spins

The reverse spin is be considered more of a control exercise than an audience trick. To an audience a reverse spin cascade looks the same as a regular cascade; however, the coordination you will learn from this trick will prove invaluable in the future.

Start with one club in the right hand in throwing position.

Now throw a few right hand throws to the left hand. You will notice that just as you throw, your wrist cocks the belly of the club downward, then snaps it upward and out, turning out of the hand with the last contact behing the thumb pushing down the handle to create the spinning action.

For a reverse spin, you must reverse this action. The wrist should not cock the club downward. The club should remain with the base pointing slightly upward for the release portion of the throw. As the arm lifts, the thumb is released and the spinning action comes from the upward thrust of the index finger. From the front, the trick should look like this:

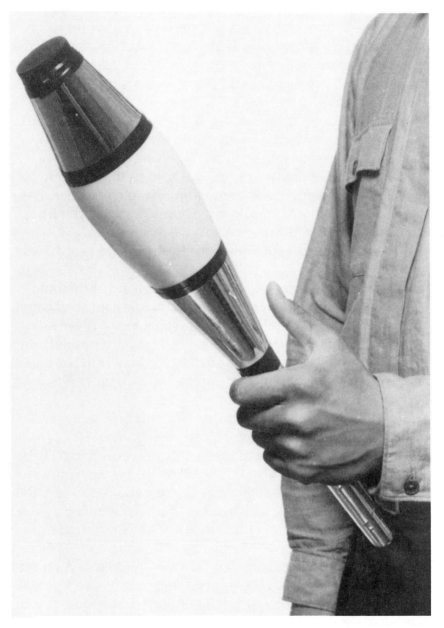

Figure 16. The throwing position of the reverse spin.

The catch of a reverse spin is also different from the normal cascade catch. The arms are held slightly higher and the palms facing outward as if you were pushing against a wall. (*See Figure 17.*)

Practice the reverse spin and catch right to left throwing a normal cascade throw back left to right. Then try the reverse spin from left to right, throwing a normal cascade throw back right to left. Repeat until you have a consistent ten throws in each direction.

Next, take one club in each hand. Place the right hand club in the reverse spin throwing position and the left hand club in the normal cascade throwing position.

Begin by throwing a right reverse spin to the left hand followed by a normal cascade throw from left to right. Then stop. Your right hand should now be in the normal cascade catch position and your left in the reverse spin catch position.

Change back to your throwing positions and repeat until smooth.

Reverse the process beginning with left hand reverse spins.

Once you have good control of the reverse spins and catch on both sides, try starting with both clubs in the reverse spin throwing position. Now the throwing and catching positions are nearly identical at all times for both hands. Work with two clubs throwing all reverse spins and catches from both hands until smooth and consistent.

Note: Watch glasses and/or teeth on this one, as the knobs of the clubs will be passing very close to your face.

Now, take three clubs and start a cascade, counting only the right hand throws. The fifth throw will be the first spin. You will catch that throw reverse spin catch. Then, throw it back into the cascade with a normal cascade throw. For now, throw only one reverse spin from the right hand then back to the cascade until consistent.

Next, reverse the process and throw a reverse spin on the fifth throw from the left hand; make the reverse catch, then, back into the left hand. Work on this until you have good control of random throws from both sides.

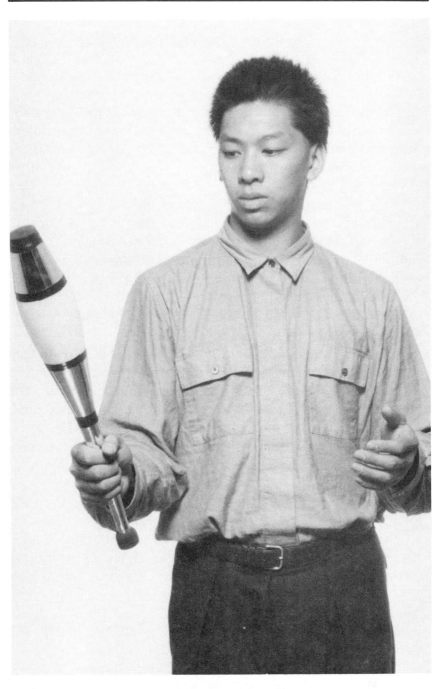

Figure 17. Reverse Spin Catch.

No Spin or The Flat Throw

The no turn or flat throw is a fairly difficult trick to learn. Although it would appear to be a very easy move, its simplicity is deceiving. The throw grip and catch grip are exactly the same as in the normal cascade, except that the wrist never cocks downward and there is no flick of the wrist. The club should always remain parallel to the ground with the base pointing out in front of you.

First, take one club in the right hand using a normal cascade grip. Now, bend your wrist slightly towards you until the club comes parallel to the ground. It is this parallel position that the club should remain during the throw. There is no flick of the wrist involved here. As the arm raises to throw the club, open the fingers leaving the palm up. The club should travel flat with no turn at all. Catch left normally and throw a normal cascade throw back to the right.

Practice throwing the flat throw to different heights to help improve control, then reverse the process and work on your left.

Next, take one club in each hand, with your right hand in the parallel throw position and your left hand in the normal throw position; throw a flat throw from right to left followed by a normal throw from left to right. Repeat until smooth, then reverse and work on the same move with the flat throw starting from your left.

Before trying three clubs, try one more exercise which will greatly help to improve your control of this trick.

Start like before, with one club in each hand, right hand in parallel grip and left hand in normal grip. This time the left will throw first followed by a flat throw from the right. Then reverse this and have the right hand throw a normal cascade throw followed by a flat throw from the left.

Mix all four methods with two clubs and try to throw the flat throws both high and low to develop good control.

Now take your third club and begin the cascade, counting your right hand throws only. The fifth right hand throw will be the first flat throw. As the fifth throw enters your right hand, quickly change to the parallel throw position and think "flat palm up" until the club is released. The club must remain parallel to the ground throughout the entire lifting motion. After this initial flat throw, the muscles in your hand may tend to want to make another flat throw. You might have experienced this same problem while learning reverse spins. Practice on the two club exercises will take care of this.

If for some reason your flat throws are not staying flat until the catch, pay particular attention to see if you are putting any unintentional wrist action on the club. Correct this by bending the wrist slightly towards or away from you keeping in mind that this adjustment must be done as the club to be thrown flat is caught in the right hand. Then, be sure to keep the club parallel to the ground throughout the lifting motion all the way until the release.

Once you have a consistent random, right hand flat throw, reverse the method for your left hand, then combine both the right and left and practice random throws from both sides.

Under the Arm

Under arm throws are very easy to learn once you have a good basic cascade. It is also an excellent audience trick and despite its simplicity is used on stage by nearly every professional club juggler.

The throw and catch are exactly the same as in a normal cascade, except that the throw will be made from under the opposite forearm.

To begin, take one club in your right hand in the normal throw position. Put your left arm in the normal catch position. As you make the throw from the right hand, move your right arm far left and under your left forearm. At the same time, move your left arm slightly to the right over your right forearm. By the time the club releases from your hand your arms should be crossed left over right, at the forearms on the left of your body.

When the club is released, the arms quickly uncross and the club is caught normally in the left hand. Reverse this method

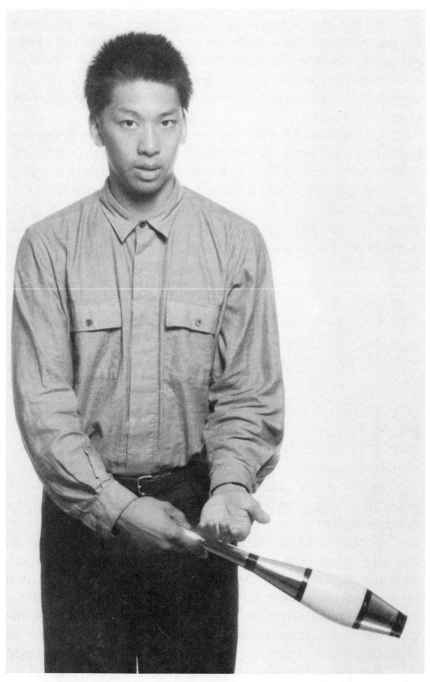

Figure 18. Top View of Underarm Throw (*right throw under left*).

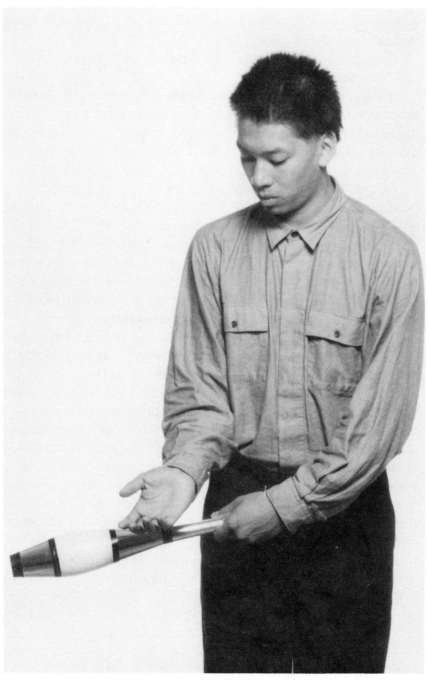

Figure 19. Top view. Left throw under right on right side of body.

and throw with the left hand, this time under the right forearm to a right hand catch. The throw will be made with the arms crossed left. (*See Figure 19.*)

Repeat both sides until you have smooth transitions and good control.

A very important point to remember in learning this trick is that when throwing under the left arm with the right hand, bring the right hand across the body to the left arm; the left arm can move slightly right but should move more than one fourth of the way across, and vice versa.

Now take one club in each and in normal cascade throwing position. The first throw will be from the right hand under the left forearm. Bring the right hand across your body and under the left forearm and release. As soon as this release is complete, throw your normal left hand throw. Now, with your (free) left hand reach quickly over and catch the club thrown under the arm. The right arm uncrosses to catch the club thrown from the left . Now reverse, and work on your left side.

The basic mechanics of this exercise should come to you fairly easily, but expect to feel quite awkward at first. Smooth flowing transitions will take many hours of practice.

Once you have good control of the two club exercise, take your third club and start a cascade counting every right hand throw. The fifth throw will be under the arm. As you cascade leading up to the fifth throw, move the cascade to the left a little to give your right hand a slight head start towards that side of your body. Make the throw, recover the cascade, and again move the pattern left. Once your right arm gets used to the long distances it has to travel to make the throw, you will no longer need to shift your pattern. Reverse this method for left side and practice hard on random throws from either side until your transitions are smooth and your catches in even tempo.

Dips

If you have spent a good deal of time on the preceeding tricks and have a pretty good cascade, you will really get a lot of enjoyment out of learning this trick. The dip is a great all around trick. It is great for audiences, easy to learn, and a good warm up for the wrists and fingers. I personally use this trick back stage in preparation for my shows because of the good general workout it gives my lower arms.

Note: Watch out for glasses and/or teeth as you do this, because the clubs pass very close to your face.

Take one club in the right hand in the normal cascade grip and stand in front of a wall (or mirror if possible). In a dip the club is thrown backhanded or palm down across the body, parallel to the wall, as opposed to a normal cascade where the club is thrown palm up nearly perpendicular to the wall.

The change in grip from normal to backhanded is accomplished by an inward rollover of the hand, bending the wrist downward. The throw is made on the upward snap of the wrist from this position.

First practice the inward rollover of the wrist from the normal cascade grip to the palm down Dip throw grip; then cock the club downward so that the base of the club points to your feet. Snap the club up and release for a throw to your left hand. The left hand catch is about the same as a normal catch. Reverse this method and repeat throwing left to right.

At first the club will go either too high or too far left or right and you will find yourself really stretching to catch it. Adjust your throws so that the club does not travel more than one foot vertically and one and a half feet horizontally. Repeat your throws left and right until you have a smooth flowing, non-stop pattern. Be sure your dip throws remain parallel to the wall and that your transistion from normal catch to throw grip is smooth and complete with the base of the club pointing to your feet before each release.

The dip throw looks like this:

Figure 20. Throw grip for Dips.

Now take one club in each hand both in the normal cascade catch position. We will throw a dip from the right to left and then a normal cascade throw from left to right—catch left/catch right, and stop. The tempo for release will be the same as a normal cascade, with the left hand throw coming just as the dip throw reaches its highest point. You will find at first that the two clubs will be passing very close to one another. If your timing is not correct, your clubs will collide, so it is important to have an even throw/catch tempo for this exercise. Practice this throwing the first dip throw with both right and left hands until you are comfortable with both sides, then get your third club.

Start your cascade and, as before, count only your right hand throws. The fifth throw from the right will be the first dip throw. Note: Be careful the clubs don't hit your face, as they come very close during this trick.

At first, the Dip throw will feel out of syncopation with the rest of your cascade, so adjust the Dip throw so it travels the same vertical and horizontal distance as your regular cascade throws. Also, stand facing a wall so you can be sure the dip throw is parallel to it. After your first dip throw, recover a smooth cascade and try again until you have good control of random throws from the right side. Then try left and work hard until you have smooth and consistent random throws from each side.

Overhead Throws

Overhead throws are another great audience trick, and quite easy to learn. However, the throw and catch are quite different than in the normal cascade. The idea is to pull one club out of the cascade and "lob" it overhead and back down into the pattern.

To start, take one club in the right hand in the normal catch position. Now raise the club up and back bending the wrist so that the club belly is about 2 inches from your right ear. The throwing action will start from here. Imagine the throw like this: you have a knife in your right hand and want to throw it overhand, end-over-end, into a point in the ceiling about one foot in front of you. The club throwing position looks like this:

Figure 21. Overhead Throwing Position.

Figure 22. Overhead Catch Position.

The throw should be a short lob with one slow turn of the club. You will throw the club on a slight right-to-left angle and it will be caught in the left hand about shoulder high, hand out and palm up, as seen in Figure 22.

Try one overhead throw right to left, then a normal cascade throw, left to right. Repeat this on the right side, until you have fair control and do not have to reach too far for the catch.

I think that you will find that while the overhead throw takes a good amount of effort to get in place, the overhead catch easily flows back into position for the normal cascade throw.

Once you are comfortable, try throwing higher, slower turning throws of various heights. This will greatly improve control. Then reverse the process and work on your left hand.

Next, take one club in each hand, both in the normal cascade catch position. Bring the right hand up and make an overhead throw. As that throw reaches its highest point, release the left hand normal cascade throw to the right, then reach up, hand out palm up, for the overhead. Catch left, then reach down for normal cascade catch right and stop.

Repeat this exercise both right and left, until smooth, then practice throwing overhead throws to varying heights to improve control.

Before going on to three clubs, try this one more exercise, which is only slightly different that what you have just done.

With one club in each hand, both in normal cascade throwing positions, you will again be making the overhead throw with the right hand, only this time begin with the normal cascade throw from left to right. As it reaches its highest point, snatch up the right hand to the overhead throw position beside the right ear and release. Quickly bring your right hand down to catch right, raise your left hand to catch left, and stop. If you don't have enough time to get your right hand down to catch the following club, throw that first left hand normal cascade throw, higher and slower turning. This will give you more time in which to make this tricky transition from throw to catch.

Now take your third club and begin a high, slow cascade, counting every right hand throw. The fifth throw from the right will be the overhead throw. The hard part will be getting that fifth club up into throwing postion beside your right ear and released in time to return and catch the cascade throw that's coming from the left hand. The fifth throw club must be snatched upward from cascade directly into the beside the ear position, then as it is released, the right hand must go down quickly to make the next catch.

Note: Be careful to keep that snatched fifth throw club well to the right of your head; as in the early learning stages of this trick, it is very easy to hit yourself in this face learning this trick.

In comparison to the throw, the overhead catch should be quite easy and you should not have any problem getting back into the cascade on your left side at least. The problem area, I am sure, will be the right side, so be sure to give extra practice to this aspect of the trick, and remember that by starting with a high, slow cascade you will have more time to complete this tricky move.

If you have a great deal of trouble with this part of the trick, try making the left hand throw before the overhead throw even higher and slower than the rest of your cascade throws. This will give you even more time.

Work on both sides until you have good control of random throws, then try throwing the overhead throws with varying, slower turning heights. I have seen this trick used many times in shows by jugglers where overhead throws would reach up to 20 feet high. With a high throw of more than a few feet, the tempo of your juggling is interrupted. In this case, once the high throw is made, the other two clubs are merely caught and held until the high club returns and the regular tempo is established again.

Lateral Overhead Throws

The lateral overhead throw is yet another excellent audience trick and looks quite different than the normal overhead throw because the club thrown laterally overhead travels a far greater amount of distance than the club thrown normally overhead. It is always seen in profile by the audience.

To begin, take one club and stand facing a wall (or mirror)

with the club in the right hand, palm up, arm extended to the 3 o'clock position as seen from the rear, elbow slightly bent out. (*See Figure 23.*)

The hand grip is the same as the normal cascade throw grip. The club will be thrown from this position with one turn overhead about 1½ feet, remaining parallel to the wall until it is caught slightly above shoulder height, palm up, in the left hand as shown in Figure 24.

I think you will find that both throwing and catching positions on both sides will flow comfortably into one another.

Try one lateral overhead throw from right to left, then return the club to the right by a normal cascade throw. Repeat this many times until you have fair control.

Hint: You are probably having some trouble catching the handle end of the club with the left hand. This is probably due to overspinning the club as the distance this club is covering is a great deal more, hand to hand, than any of the previous tricks. If this is your problem, slow the spin by pushing up with the right palm and give the throw a little less wrist action.

Once you are comfortable with right throws, reverse the exercise and work on the left, then practice throwing higher, slower turning lateral overhead throws from each side in order to improve good control.

Now take two clubs, one in each hand, both in the normal cascade throwing position. Make a lateral overhead throw from right to left; then, as that throw comes directly overhead, take a normal cascade throw left to right, reach up and catch left, reach down and catch right and stop.

Next, try this exercise which is only slightly different from what you have just done.

Start with one club in each hand and again you will make a lateral overhead throw with the right hand, only this time begin with the left to right normal cascade throw, as it reaches its highest point reach up and release the lateral overhead throw from right to left, then reach down and catch right, and reach up to catch left and stop.

Practice hard on these two exercises, being sure to keep the lateral overhead throw parallel to the wall, then reverse the exer-

Figure 23. Lateral Overhead Throw Start Position.

Figure 24. Lateral Overhead Throw Catch Position.

cise and work on your left side.

Now take your three clubs and start a high, slow cascade counting every right hand throw. The fifth throw will be the first lateral overhead throw. You will probably find it hard at first to release that throw quick enough to get your right hand down to catch the following club, but it should not be nearly as difficult as trick #9. You will find the catches will flow smoothly back into throwing position.

Work on random throws from the right, then reverse this method for the left until you have good control of random throws from both sides.

As with trick #9, you can achieve better control of lateral overhead throws of varying heights.

This trick can be done with continuous throws from either side with single or double throws or with continuous throws from *both* sides.

Ending Note: Remember to practice your bad side.

Basic
Fancy
Starts

Once you have a routine established, it is always nice to have a fancy start and finish. I'll give you two of each. At first, work on sections of your routine, and consider dividing it up into three or four parts; then, work hard to perform it completely through without a mistake; and, be sure to include a start and finish.

Club Balance Start

First take one club in each hand. Place the knob of the left club on the belly of the right club so that the left club balances vertically on the right, as shown in Figure 25.

Practice balancing the club on club until you have fair control. Then try lifting and pulling the right club so that the balanced club makes one reverse spin to a catch in the left hand. The right club remains in the right hand.

Get good control of this thowing motion before moving on, and don't worry if you can only keep the balance for only a short time. A balance of three seconds is all that's necessary for this trick, although once you learn it I am sure you will want to hold it a little longer.

Next, take two clubs in the left and one in the right. Use either of the clubs in the left for the balance. Once it is in the balanced position, return the left hand to normal throwing position and throw the balanced club with a reverse spin to the left hand. As this throw reaches its highest point, start the cascade

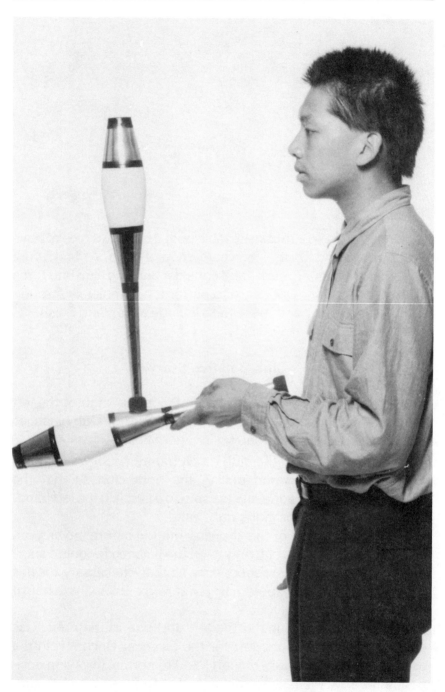

Figure 25. Balance Club on Club.

Figure 26. Chin Balance.

just as you would during a normal reverse spin trick. If you learned the reverse spins well, earlier in this book, you should have no trouble with this one.

Chin Balance Start

For this trick you will need fair control of a chin balance. Place the knob of the club in the hollow of your chin with head bent slightly back as shown in Figure 26.

Keep your knees slightly bent and feet apart because you will need some mobility to stay under the club. Focus your eye and attention on the uppermost part of the club that you can see. Use your hands to place the club into a balance. It will take some time to learn which way is actually vertical when looking at the club from this position. As you feel and see the club move in any direction, compensate by moving the chin in the same direction until the club goes back to the balance. At first you will have a great deal of front/back and side-to-side movement, but soon you will find that these movements will refine into minute adjustments, not noticeable by anyone.

Again, only a three second balance is necessary to do this trick, so once you can hold it that long, get your other two clubs. With two clubs left and one right, balance one of the left two on your chin and return your left hand to throwing position. Once you are ready to start the cascade, let the balanced club fall to the front and slightly to the right. As the knob leaves your chin throw the right club to begin the cascade. Adjust the angle of fall of the balanced club so that it lands comfortably in your right hand. Once you have a good balance, this trick is very easy.

FOUR

Basic
Fancy
Finishes

The Three Club Catch/Finish

The three club catch finish is very easy to learn. All you have to do is stop throwing with your left and catch instead until all three clubs are in your left hand. Any person with normal-sized hands should have little trouble holding three clubs in one hand. Persons with smaller hands may have to work a bit harder at it.

Start by holding two clubs left and one club right. Throw the right club with one turn to the left and catch it on top of the two clubs you already have. By keeping your left elbow out at the time of the catch, you will have a better catching angle for the third club. This gets the knobs of the first two clubs out of the way of the knob of the second club. The thumb and first finger grips the first two clubs while the three remaining fingers open to accept the third club.

Practice this awhile and then start your cascade, and end with a three club finish. Catch all three clubs on top of the other as they come into the left hand as shown in Figure 27.

One Between Two Catch/Finish

This finish is also very easy to learn and involves catching the handle of the last club between two clubs held in your left hand, as shown in Figure 28.

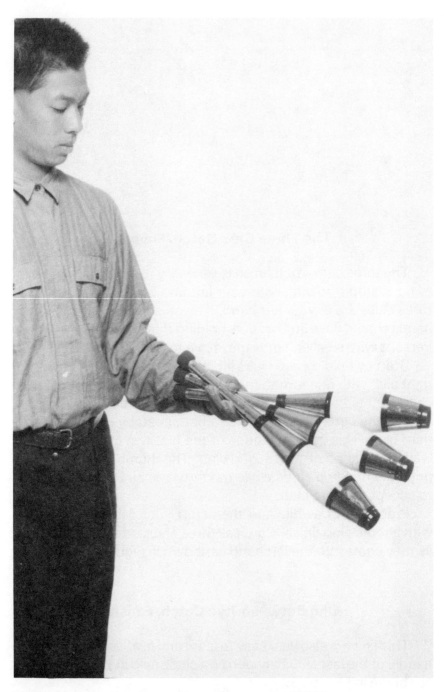

Figure 27. Three Club, One Hand Finish.

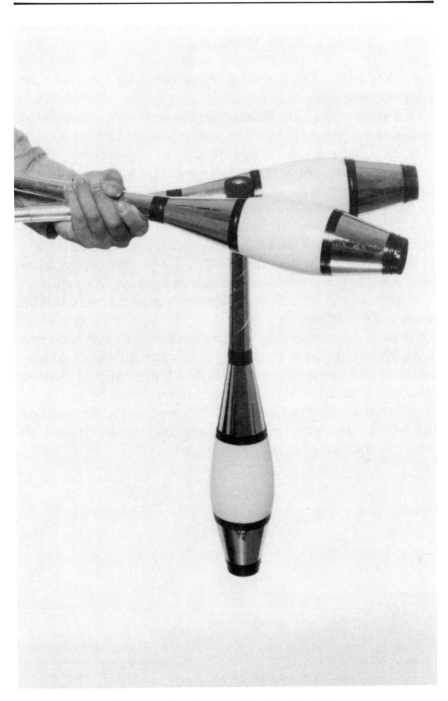

Figure 28. One Between Two Catch/Finish.

Begin with two clubs in the left hand held slightly loose in the normal throwing position. Using your thumb and fingers, try to open and close the bellies of the clubs much like you would do with chopsticks. Once you have this movement, throw your third club with your right hand with one spin to your left hand. As the knob of the right club passes the vertical point, open the bellies of the two left clubs and stab at the neck of the coming right club. As the right club contacts the upper bellies of the other two clubs, squeeze the left hand tightly to keep it from slipping out.

Note: this trick is much easier when using clubs with a large knob. If you are having trouble and think that the last club is slipping out because the knob is to small, try wrapping the knob of one of your clubs with tape so that it is larger than the other two; then, be sure that is the last club you throw! The change in balance and weight will be insignificant and the trick will be much more secure.

Now start a three club cascade and stop by catching two clubs in the left. Delay the last right hand throw slightly to give you time to arrange the two left clubs for the stabbing motion. Now throw the last right throw, stab and squeeze.

You can make this finish a little easier by catching the first two left clubs closer to the knobs, and then throw the last club from the right with a higher, slower turn.

CONCLUSION

Now that you have the 10 Basic 3 Club Tricks and a fancy start and finish under your belt, what are you going to do with them?

Try to arrange a routine where you perform each trick, for at least 10 throws in given order. Begin with a fancy start and end with a fancy finish.

If you have enjoyed yourself thus far and want to learn more about club juggling, performing, or just juggling in general, look for future titles available soon from Dick Franco.

Paul Bachman "Prince of Jugglers

Bobby May

Dick Franco

Kit Summers

Billy Tirko

Stone and Lind 1904

Harry Lind 1904

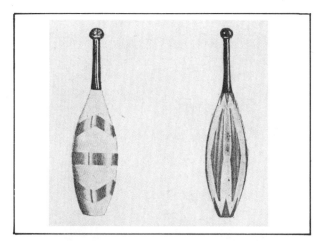

Clubs by Edward Van Wyck Catalog 1935

Five Juggling Jewels

Bobby May

Tommy Breen

To MY PAL
  BOBBY MAY:
— ALWAYS A SOURCE
OF INSPIRATION TO ME
BOTH AS A PERSON AND
A PERFORMER!
  BEST LUCK
    ALWAYS
    Gil Dova

Gil Dova

Gerdi Stern

Truzzi

Three Swifts

Alburtus and Bartrum 1899

Kathi Gultini

The Five Elgins

Gerd Brothers

Gerd Brothers

Gerd Brothers

Dennis Soldati

Bobby May-17 years old

David Lucas

Torianis

Three Houcs

Three Houcs

Don and Lana Reed

Bobby May Skating Vanities 1942

Dick Franco Italy 1980

The Half Brothers

Suzanne Zsilak

Suzanne and Fudi

Dick Franco Cafe Versailles, New York 1982

Rudenko Brothers

Ellen Dea

Herman Ripa 1939

Joe Boyle

Joe Boyle

Tommy Breen

Margrit Ginotti

Gil Dova

Reverho

Rudenko Brothers

Dieto

Max Morland 1944

Pierre Bal

Carter Brown